INSECTS AROUND THE WORLD

ALL ABOUT NORTH AMERICAN GRASSHOPPERS

EZ READERS

Annette Whipple

Creating Young Nonfiction Readers

EZ Readers lets children delve into nonfiction at beginning reading levels. Young readers are introduced to new concepts, facts, ideas, and vocabulary.

Tips for Reading Nonfiction with Beginning Readers

Talk about Nonfiction

Begin by explaining that nonfiction books give us information that is true. The book will be organized around a specific topic or idea, and we may learn new facts through reading.

Look at the Parts

Most nonfiction books have helpful features. Our *EZ Readers* include color photographs and graphic aids, a table of contents, a glossary, and an index. Share the purpose of these features with your reader.

Color Photos and Graphic Aids

A lot of information can be found by "reading" photos, charts, maps, and other graphic aids found within nonfiction texts. Help your reader learn more about the different ways information can be displayed.

Table of Contents

Located at the front of the book, this list shows the big ideas within the text and the page numbers where they can be found.

Glossary

Located at the back of the book, the glossary defines key words and phrases that are related to the topic. These words and phrases can be found in the text in colored type.

Index

Located at the back of the book, an index is an alphabetical list of topics and the page numbers where they can be found.

With a little help and guidance about reading nonfiction, you can feel good about introducing a young reader to the world of *EZ Readers* nonfiction books.

Mitchell Lane
PUBLISHERS

2001 SW 31st Avenue
Hallandale, FL 33009
www.mitchelllane.com

First Edition, 2025.

Author: Annette Whipple
Designer: Rhea Magaro
Editor: Kim Thompson

Names/credits:
Title: All About North American Grasshoppers / by Annette Whipple
Description: Hallandale, FL : Mitchell Lane Publishers, [2025]

Series: Insects Around the World
Library bound ISBN: 978-1-68020-956-3
eBook ISBN: 978-1-68020-959-4

EZ Readers is an imprint of Mitchell Lane Publishers

PHOTO CREDITS
iStock: DANIEL RIECK, cover; marcophotos, 1; Shutterstock: Dmytro Khlystun, 4-5; Protasov AN, 6-7; Vera Larina, 8-9; Richard Cook, 10-11; Tomohiro Ishiga, 12-13; Angga Andriyan, 14-15; Galina Gorkavay, 16-17; Kirill I, 18-19; Special Beauty, 20-21; nblx, 22; Blue Planet Studio, 22; andyborow, 22; Galyna Andrushko, 22

Paperback ISBN: 979-8-89260-144-3

CONTENTS

Grasshoppers live around the world. These **insects** can live in many different **habitats**, from wet rainforests to dry deserts. About 400 **species** of grasshoppers live in North America. Each species looks a little different. Many are green or brown. Some are long and lean. Others are short and round.

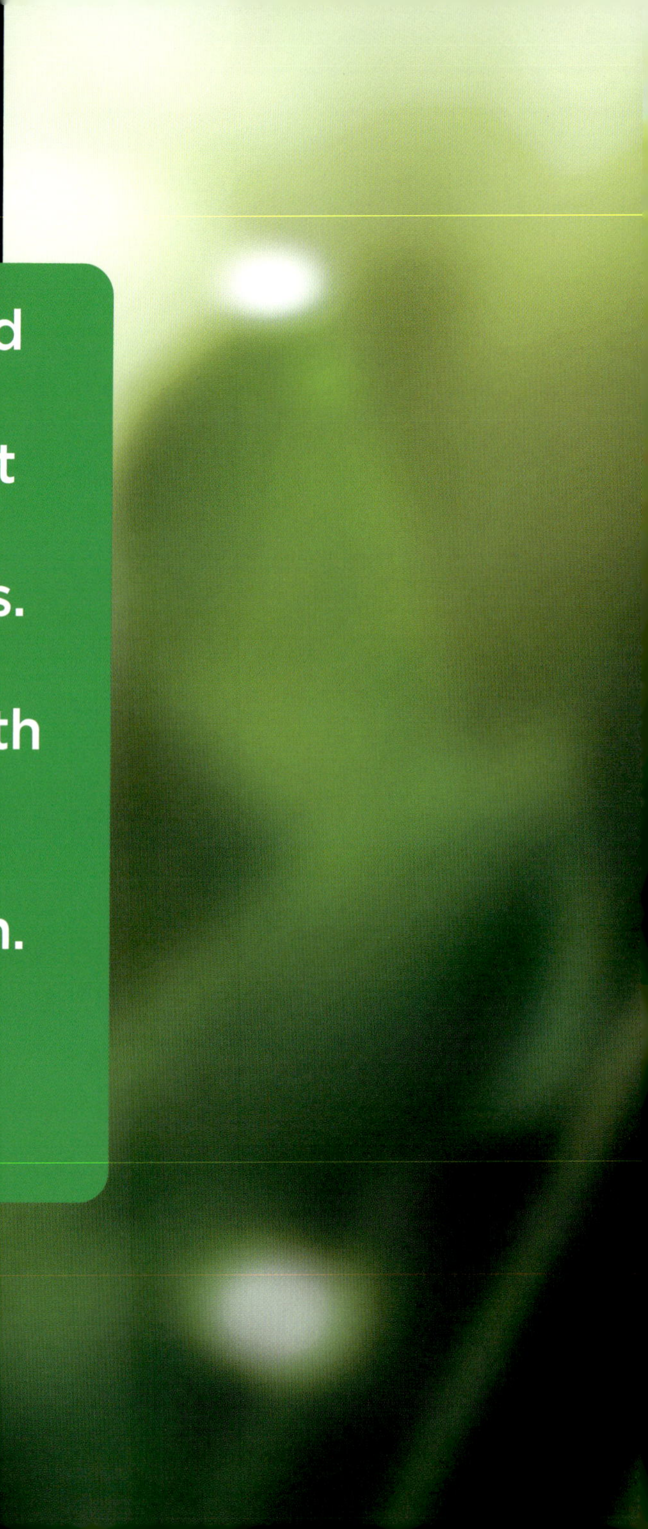

Grasshoppers use their strong legs to leap. They can also fly. Usually, they don't fly very far. But sometimes a **swarm** of grasshoppers flies more than 50 miles (80 kilometers) in a day.

Grasshoppers use their large eyes to find food. They use their **antennae** to smell and touch. They taste with their mouths. They have eardrums near their hind legs! They rub their legs on their wings to make chirping sounds and talk to other grasshoppers.

Grasshoppers must watch out for **predators**. Birds, frogs, and snakes like to eat grasshoppers. Some people also eat grasshoppers.

A female grasshopper lays hundreds of eggs in a year. She lays her eggs in the soil inside a case called a pod. A pod can have 100 eggs. Pods protect eggs from heat, cold, and water.

Young grasshoppers hatch from eggs in the spring. They are called **nymphs**. Nymphs look like tiny adults, but they don't yet have wings. In time, their wings grow.

Grasshoppers eat plants. A lot of plants! Their strong jaws and teeth chew through all kinds of leaves, stems, and stalks.

Grasshoppers can be **pests**. They eat crops. Usually, they do not cause too much harm. But sometimes, a grasshopper swarm eats every plant in an area. This can destroy whole farms.

Grasshoppers are also helpful. They break down plants so that new plants can grow. They provide food for many animals. They help nature stay in balance.

WHERE DO GRASSHOPPERS LIVE?

Grasshoppers live all over North America. You can find them in these habitats.

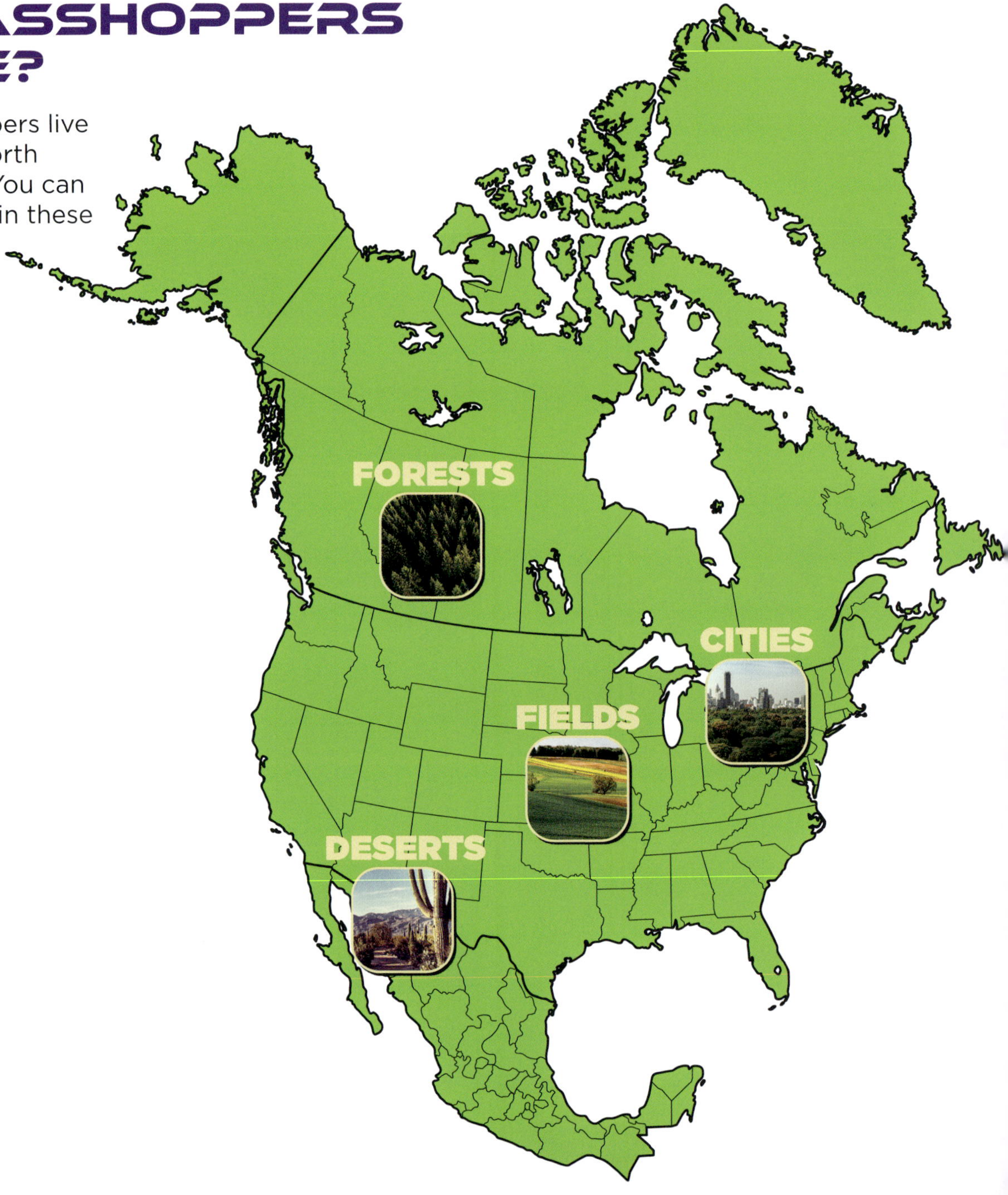

INTERESTING FACTS

- The wingspans of some grasshoppers can be 10 inches (25 centimeters) long.
- Grasshoppers can leap 20 times their own body length.
- Grasshoppers are also called locusts.
- People eat grasshoppers dried, jellied, and roasted.
- Grasshoppers were on Earth before dinosaurs.
- Grasshoppers protect themselves by spitting brown liquid.

PARTS OF A GRASSHOPPER

Eyes
Grasshoppers have five eyes: three small eyes that detect light and two large, compound eyes made up of many lenses.

Mandibles
Strong jaws called mandibles help grasshoppers chew through tough plants.

Spiracles
Air enters the grasshopper's body through holes along its sides called spiracles.

Tympana
Oval-shaped structures above the hind legs, called tympana, act like eardrums to hear sounds.

Wings
Grasshoppers have two hard, protective wings and two flying wings.

GLOSSARY

antennae (an-TEN-ee)
Feelers on the head of an insect

habitats (HAB-i-tats)
Areas where animals and plants usually live

insects (IN-sekts)
Small animals with hard outer skeletons, six legs, and three body sections

nymphs (nimfz)
Young insects that become adults by shedding skin

pests (pests)
Insects or other animals that cause destruction and damage, especially on farms

predators (PRED-uh-turz)
Animals that hunt and eat other animals

species (SPEE-sheez)
One type or kind of living thing; members of the same species can have babies

swarm (sworm)
A large group of insects that gather and move together

INDEX

FURTHER READING

French, Jess. *The Book of Brilliant Bugs.* New York, NY: DK Publishing, 2020.

McDonald, Jill. *Exploring Insects.* New York, NY: Doubleday, 2023.

ON THE INTERNET

Animal Corner: Grasshopper
https://animalcorner.org/animals/grasshopper
Learn lots of details about grasshoppers at this fact-filled website.

AZ Animals: 10 Incredible Grasshopper Facts
https://a-z-animals.com/blog/10-incredible-grasshopper-facts
Read 10 fascinating facts about grasshoppers.